An Infographic Guide to

LONDON

written by
Simon Holland

designed by
Peter Clayman

First published in 2016 by Wayland
Copyright © Wayland, 2016

Produced for Wayland by DUTCH&DANE

All rights reserved.

Written by Simon Holland
Cover and inside design by Peter Clay
Edited by Corinne Lucas

ISBN: 978 0 7502 9954 1

Wayland, an imprint of
Hachette Children's Group
Part of Hodder and Stoughton
Carmelite House
50 Victoria Embankment
London EC4Y 0DZ

An Hachette UK Company
www.hachette.co.uk
www.hachettechildrens.co.uk

Printed in China

10 9 8 7 6 5 4 3 2 1

Picture acknowledgements (cover and inside pages): All images and graphic
elements used in the illustrations are courtesy of Shutterstock, with the exception
of page 54 (bottom left): all London football club badges (as vector graphics)
sourced via Wikimedia Commons.

Every attempt has been made to clear copyright. Should there be any inadvertent
omission, please apply to the publisher for rectification.

The website addresses (URLs) included in this book were valid at the time of going
to press. However, it is possible that contents or addresses may have changed
since the publication of this book. No responsibility for any such changes can
be accepted by either the author or the Publisher.

Contents

Welcome to London!

When visiting – or even just thinking about – such a huge and historic city, it's tricky to know where to start. To get you on the move, here are a few basic facts about London.

LONDON FACT FILE

- CAPITAL CITY OF THE UK
- UK POPULATION: more than 64 million people
- POPULATION OF LONDON: more than 8.6 million people
- TOTAL AREA OF GREATER LONDON: 1,572 square kilometres
- AREA FIRST INHABITED: in around 3500 BCE

The UNITED KINGDOM (or UK, for short) is made up of four countries: ENGLAND, SCOTLAND, WALES and NORTHERN IRELAND.

You can visit royal residences in Central London, such as Buckingham Palace and St James's Palace, where the current monarch of the United Kingdom – Queen Elizabeth II – lives and works (see pages 34–35).

Buckingham Palace

The Houses of Parliament, Westminster

Wembley Stadium

WEST LONDON

Kensing

There have been royal buildings in Westminster since the 10th century. It's also the home of the UK Parliament (see pages 20–21).

Battersea Power Station

Some of the buildings from London's industrial past now have a different purpose: the Bankside Power Station houses the Tate Modern art gallery (see pages 33 and 62), while the Battersea Power Station is being converted into luxury flats and leisure facilities.

SCOTLAND

NORTHERN IRELAND

Glasgow

Edinburgh

Belfast

Dublin

ENGLAND

WALES

Cardiff

LONDON

REPUBLIC OF IRELAND

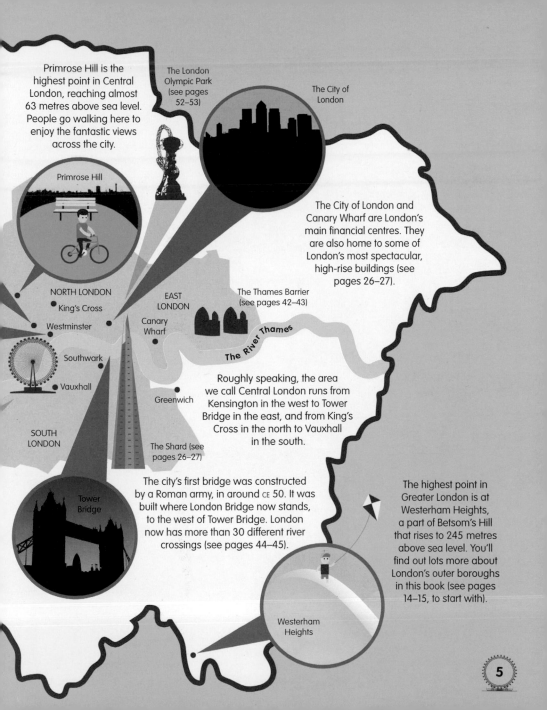

Primrose Hill is the highest point in Central London, reaching almost 63 metres above sea level. People go walking here to enjoy the fantastic views across the city.

Primrose Hill

The London Olympic Park (see pages 52–53)

The City of London

The City of London and Canary Wharf are London's main financial centres. They are also home to some of London's most spectacular, high-rise buildings (see pages 26–27).

NORTH LONDON

King's Cross

Westminster

EAST LONDON

Canary Wharf

The Thames Barrier (see pages 42–43)

Southwark

Vauxhall

The River Thames

Greenwich

Roughly speaking, the area we call Central London runs from Kensington in the west to Tower Bridge in the east, and from King's Cross in the north to Vauxhall in the south.

SOUTH LONDON

The Shard (see pages 26–27)

Tower Bridge

The city's first bridge was constructed by a Roman army, in around CE 50. It was built where London Bridge now stands, to the west of Tower Bridge. London now has more than 30 different river crossings (see pages 44–45).

The highest point in Greater London is at Westerham Heights, a part of Betsom's Hill that rises to 245 metres above sea level. You'll find out lots more about London's outer boroughs in this book (see pages 14–15, to start with).

Westerham Heights

A London timeline

It took thousands of years for London to grow into the sprawling metropolis it is today. This timeline will introduce you to some of the people and events that played a part in the city's development.

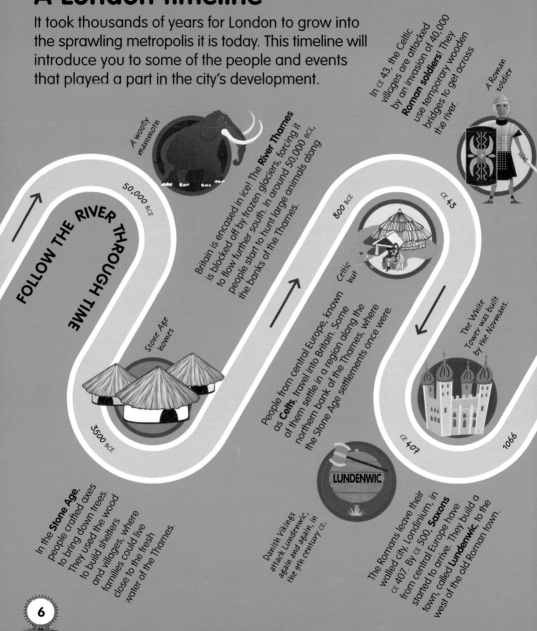

A woolly mammoth

A Roman soldier

Celtic hut

FOLLOW THE RIVER THROUGH TIME

Stone Age homes

50,000 BCE

Britain is encased in ice! The **River Thames** is blocked off by frozen glaciers, forcing it to flow further south. In around 50,000 BCE, people start to hunt large animals along the banks of the Thames.

3500 BCE

In the **Stone Age**, people crafted axes to bring down trees. They used the wood to build shelters and villages, where families could live close to the fresh water of the Thames.

800 BCE

People from central Europe, known as **Celts**, travel into Britain. Some of them settle in a region along the northern bank of the Thames, where the Stone Age settlements once were.

CE 43

In CE 43, the Celtic villages are attacked by an invasion of 40,000 **Roman soldiers!** They use temporary wooden bridges to get across the river.

The White Tower was built by the Normans.

1066

CE 407

The Romans leave their walled city, Londinium, in CE 407. By CE 500, **Saxons** from central Europe have started to arrive. They build a town, called **Lundenwic**, to the west of the old Roman town.

LUNDENWIC

Danish Vikings attack Lundenwic, again and again, in the 9th century CE.

In 1066, **William the Conqueror** (a duke from Normandy in France) leads an army into England and then defeats the last of the Anglo-Saxon kings. He builds a stone castle in London to defend the city.

William Shakespeare (1564–1616)

The Great Fire of 1666 destroys most of medieval London

Olympic flame

1558–1603

1666

1908, 1948 and 2012

In the age of **Queen Elizabeth I**, theatres are built on the south side of the Thames. **William Shakespeare** also has one here, called the Globe.

Britain is at war with Germany from 1939 to 1945 (Second World War). The city comes under attack from aerial bombing raids in 1940–41, a time known as **the Blitz**. Many London homes and lives are destroyed.

London is now a true Olympic city. It has been chosen to host the **Summer Olympic Games** three times – in 1908, 1948 and 2012.

The Blitz

A 21st-century Tube train

The 1800s

1940

Today ...

In 1825, London is the largest city in the world, with a population of around 1.75 million.

Gas lamps start to light the streets in 1809, and the **Underground trains** start running in 1863. By 1900, **electricity** is a new source of power in the city.

Today, London is one of the most famous and most visited cities in the world. The city is now home to more than **8.6 million people.**

7

Dates that changed a city

London is no stranger to triumph and disaster! For many centuries, it's been at the centre of major changes, political events and terrible acts of war. Here are some of the things that have made a great impact on the city.

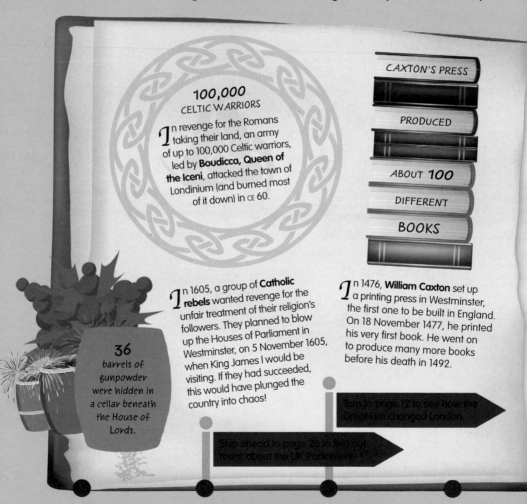

100,000 CELTIC WARRIORS

In revenge for the Romans taking their land, an army of up to 100,000 Celtic warriors, led by **Boudicca, Queen of the Iceni**, attacked the town of Londinium (and burned most of it down) in CE 60.

CAXTON'S PRESS PRODUCED ABOUT 100 DIFFERENT BOOKS

36 barrels of gunpowder were hidden in a cellar beneath the House of Lords.

In 1605, a group of **Catholic rebels** wanted revenge for the unfair treatment of their religion's followers. They planned to blow up the Houses of Parliament in Westminster, on 5 November 1605, when King James I would be visiting. If they had succeeded, this would have plunged the country into chaos!

In 1476, **William Caxton** set up a printing press in Westminster, the first one to be built in England. On 18 November 1477, he printed his very first book. He went on to produce many more books before his death in 1492.

Turn to page 12 to see how the Great Fire changed London.

Skip ahead to page 20 to find out more about the UK Parliament.

20 JANUARY 1265: First Parliament (government) meeting at Westminster Hall.

4–5 NOVEMBER 1605: Guy Fawkes is arrested beneath the Houses of Parliament.

2 SEPTEMBER 1666: The Great Fire began within the walls of the City of London.

23 OCTOBER 1707: First Parliament held involving MPs from all over Great Britain.

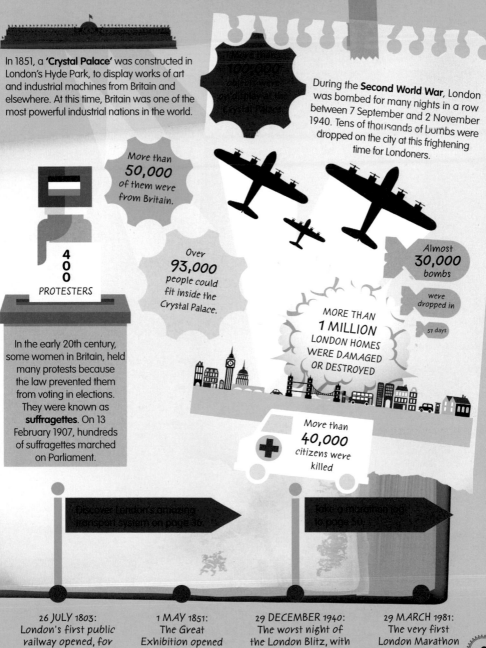

In 1851, a **'Crystal Palace'** was constructed in London's Hyde Park, to display works of art and industrial machines from Britain and elsewhere. At this time, Britain was one of the most powerful industrial nations in the world.

More than 100,000 objects were on display at the Crystal Palace.

During the **Second World War**, London was bombed for many nights in a row between 7 September and 2 November 1940. Tens of thousands of bombs were dropped on the city at this frightening time for Londoners.

More than **50,000** of them were from Britain.

Over **93,000** people could fit inside the Crystal Palace.

Almost **30,000** bombs

were dropped in

57 days

MORE THAN **1 MILLION** LONDON HOMES WERE DAMAGED OR DESTROYED

4 0 0
PROTESTERS

In the early 20th century, some women in Britain, held many protests because the law prevented them from voting in elections. They were known as **suffragettes**. On 13 February 1907, hundreds of suffragettes marched on Parliament.

More than **40,000** citizens were killed

Discover London's amazing transport system on page 36.

Take a marathon leap to page 50.

26 JULY 1803:
London's first public railway opened, for moving goods.

1 MAY 1851:
The Great Exhibition opened in Hyde Park.

29 DECEMBER 1940:
The worst night of the London Blitz, with 163 people killed.

29 MARCH 1981:
The very first London Marathon took place.

Diseased London

Between 1348 and 1665 there were nearly 40 outbreaks of disease in the capital that killed many thousands of Londoners. At their worst, these outbreaks of 'plague' could wipe out around 20 per cent of the city's population.

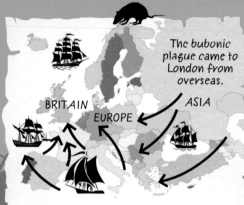

The bubonic plague came to London from overseas.

BRITAIN
EUROPE
ASIA

FLEAS BITE SICK RODENTS

INFECTED FLEAS

INFECTED RODENTS

SICK FLEAS BITE HEALTHY RODENTS

RODENT POPULATION GETS SMALLER

The bubonic plague was a disease that spread among rodents, such as black rats. Fleas on the rodents caught the disease, and then spread it by hopping on to healthy rodents and biting them. When all the sick animals starting dying, the fleas needed new 'hosts' to live on … so they started hopping on to humans. The plague reached London in the **autumn of 1348**. Within 18 months, it had **killed at least half** of all the city's residents.

Headaches

Coughing blood

Vomiting

The bubonic plague was an extremely unpleasant illness. The victims often developed painful swellings, known as buboes, which normally appeared in their neck, armpits and groin. They suffered a variety of other symptoms, too.

Fever

There was a HIGH RATE OF DEATH among those who were infected.

If you were unlucky enough to catch the disease, it was unlikely that you'd live to tell the tale.

Buboes (swellings) in the neck and groin

Bruises

Blisters

Londoners went to many lengths to try and **stop the plague** from spreading. They stayed in their homes, marked the houses that were infected – and killed stray dogs and cats in their thousands, thinking that they might be the carriers of this deadly disease.

240,000
DOGS AND CATS WERE PUT TO DEATH FROM 1664–65.

TOBACCO
WAS SMOKED TO KEEP 'BAD AIR' OUT OF PEOPLE'S LUNGS.

STRAW
WAS HUNG OUTSIDE INFECTED HOMES, AS A WARNING.

VINEGAR
WAS USED TO TRY AND 'DISINFECT' COINS USED IN TRADE.

Most people suffering with the plague died within SEVEN days:

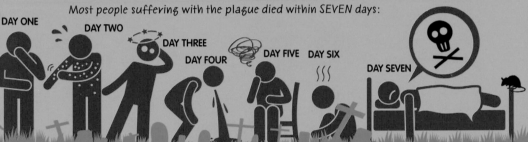

DAY ONE
DAY TWO
DAY THREE
DAY FOUR
DAY FIVE
DAY SIX
DAY SEVEN

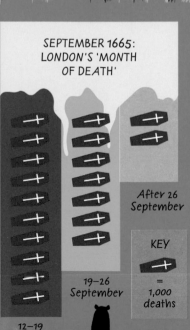

SEPTEMBER 1665: LONDON'S 'MONTH OF DEATH'

After 26 September

19–26 September

12–19 September

KEY

= 1,000 deaths

THE CITY'S MASS GRAVES AND 'PLAGUE PITS'

UP TO 200
PLAGUE VICTIMS WERE BURIED IN THE SAME MASS GRAVE.

CHILDREN
WERE BURIED IN THE SPACES BETWEEN THE ADULTS.

FIVE
PEOPLE WERE OFTEN BURIED ON TOP OF ONE ANOTHER.

The Great Fire

In September 1666, a fire began at a bakery in Pudding Lane. The blaze spread throughout the city and destroyed most of the medieval buildings inside the old Roman walls.

The Great Fire wiped out almost 90 per cent of London's old, medieval buildings.

1. The heat of the ovens created sparks.

8. Strong winds fanned the flames.

2. There were lots of wooden buildings ...

Here are the main reasons why the Fire of London spread through the city so quickly, with such devastating effects.

3. ... with dry, thatched roofs.

7. Warm, dry air fuelled the fire.

6. Buildings were coated in weatherproof 'pitch', which caught fire easily.

5. Upper floors jutted out towards each other, passing the flames from house to house.

4. The buildings were very close together, in narrow streets.

The Great Fire – a very small percentage of the population! 0.01%

Only SIX people are thought to have died in the Great Fire

- 80,000 people
- 6 people

SEPTEMBER **2**

SEPTEMBER **3**

SEPTEMBER **4**

1700°C
IS THE TEMPERATURE THE FIRE REACHED

The fire raged on **for three days**. Fire-fighters created 'fire breaks' by blowing up and pulling down buildings, to stop the flames from spreading. This didn't work very well, however ... not until the winds started to die down on **Wednesday 5 September**.

The fire began just after midnight on **Sunday 2 September 1666**. On **Tuesday 4 September**, the flames swept across most of the City of London area, destroying St Paul's and many of the churches and other important buildings around it.

87 MEDIEVAL CHURCHES DESTROYED

13,200 HOUSES BURNT

70,000 HOMELESS

The old St Paul's Cathedral, built by the Normans, was badly damaged by the blaze. A new cathedral – along with many new churches – was designed by a scientist and architect called **Sir Christopher Wren** (1632–1723).

45 YEARS needed to construct the new cathedral (1675–1720)

← **33** → METRES AWAY IS THE DISTANCE THAT A WHISPER CAN BE HEARD IN THE 'WHISPERING GALLERY' (JUST UNDERNEATH THE CATHEDRAL'S MAIN DOME)

MORE THAN **1,400** YEARS SINCE A CHURCH WAS FIRST BUILT ON THIS SITE (IN AROUND CE **604**)

36 TENNIS COURTS COULD FIT INSIDE THE CATHEDRAL

£1,095,556 WAS THE COST OF CONSTRUCTION (about £146 million in today's money)

400 BUILDERS ON SITE DURING THE PEAK TIME OF CONSTRUCTION

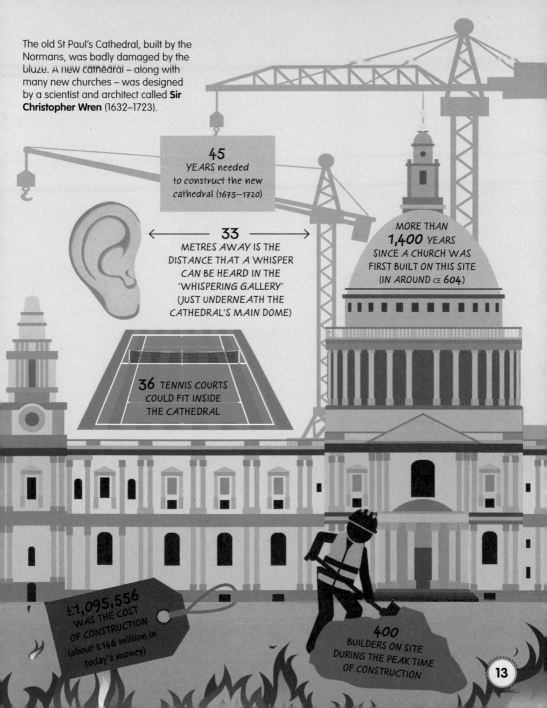

London's boroughs

Over hundreds of years, many different villages, towns and districts have grown and joined together to form what's known as Greater London. It's a vast metropolis that is now divided into 33 different districts – the City of London and 32 larger boroughs.

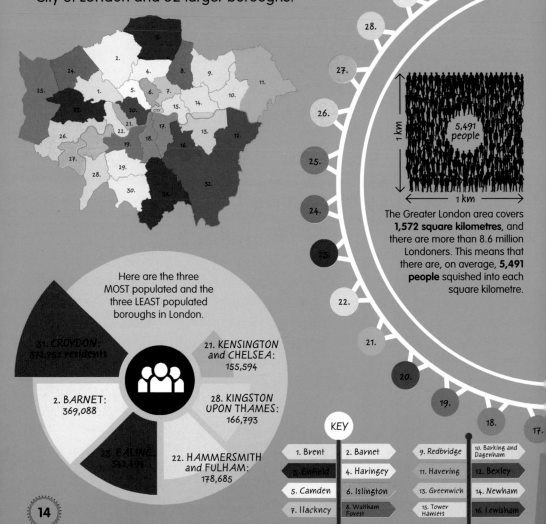

The Greater London area covers **1,572 square kilometres**, and there are more than 8.6 million Londoners. This means that there are, on average, **5,491 people** squished into each square kilometre.

1 km × 1 km = **5,491 people**

Here are the three MOST populated and the three LEAST populated boroughs in London.

31. CROYDON: 372,752 residents

2. BARNET: 369,088

13. EALING: 342,494

21. KENSINGTON and CHELSEA: 155,594

28. KINGSTON UPON THAMES: 166,793

22. HAMMERSMITH and FULHAM: 178,685

KEY

1. Brent	2. Barnet
3. Enfield	4. Haringey
5. Camden	6. Islington
7. Hackney	8. Waltham Forest

9. Redbridge	10. Barking and Dagenham
11. Havering	12. Bexley
13. Greenwich	14. Newham
15. Tower Hamlets	16. Lewisham

The **London Eye**, on the south bank of the Thames, is a giant Ferris wheel. Riding inside the pods gives passengers an excellent view of the city, in all directions. The are 32 pods, representing the city's 32 boroughs.

Many of the London boroughs have names that originally come from **Anglo-Saxon** times, from the 6th–11th century, or from earlier **Celtic** days. Some of them tell us what these areas might have been like when people first lived there.

POPULATION OF OUTER LONDON BOROUGHS: around 5.5 million

36%

64%

POPULATION OF INNER LONDON BOROUGHS: around 3.1 million

London was chopped up into boroughs in 1965, as a better way of governing the capital and looking after the needs of each area. Most of them have **between 150,000 and 300,000 people** living in them, with more in the outer boroughs.

BARNET means 'Land cleared by burning'.

HACKNEY means 'Haca's Island in the marshland'.

The River BRENT and its district are both named after a Celtic goddess called 'Brigantia'.

HARINGEY means 'Enclosure in the grey wood'.

BROMLEY means 'Clearing where broom bushes grow'.

LAMBETH means 'Landing place for lambs'.

CROYDON means either 'Valley of wild saffron' or 'Crooked valley'.

WESTMINSTER means 'Western monastery'.

SUTTON means 'Southern farming settlement'.

1.
2.
3.
4.
5.
6.
7.
8.
9.
10.
11.
12.
13.
14.
15.
16.

17. Southwark	18. Lambeth	25. Hillingdon	26. Hounslow
19. Wandsworth	20. City of Westminster	27. Richmond	28. Kingston upon Thames
21. Kensington and Chelsea	22. Hammersmith and Fulham	29. Merton	30. Sutton
23. Islington	24. Harrow	31. Croydon	32. Bromley

NEXT PAGE

London's people

London is one of the most multi-cultural and ethnically mixed places on the planet. More than 300 different languages are spoken in the city, and there are more than 50 different communities of people that have come to London from overseas.

HELLO

Bonjour ...

Chairete!

White British people: 44.9 per cent of all Londoners

London is the capital of the UK, but its people are from **many different ethnic backgrounds**. This is what makes the city so vibrant and interesting. It is shaped and influenced by all of these different cultures.

Asian-British people: 18.4%

White, non-British people: 14.9%

Black (including African, Caribbean and Black British) people: 13.3%

Other mixed race Londoners: 5%

People from other ethnic groups (including Arab and Middle Eastern people): 3.5%

Every city needs to cope with **human waste**. To deal with the waste-water created by all these millions of people, there are thousands of kilometres of sewage pipes running underneath London's streets.

There are more than ...

... 16,000 KILOMETRES of sewage pipes.

4.4 BILLION litres of London waste-water are flushed ...

... through the pipes each day ...

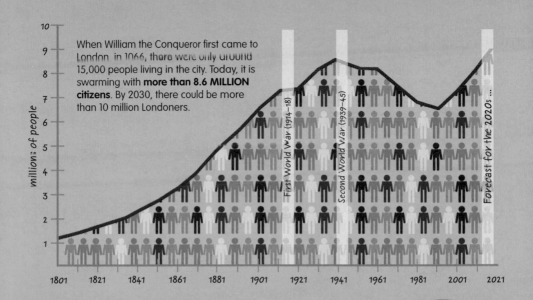

When William the Conqueror first came to London in 1066, there were only around 15,000 people living in the city. Today, it is swarming with **more than 8.6 MILLION citizens**. By 2030, there could be more than 10 million Londoners.

millions of people

First World War (1914–18)

Second World War (1939–45)

Forecast for the 2020s …

1801 1821 1841 1861 1881 1901 1921 1941 1961 1981 2001 2021

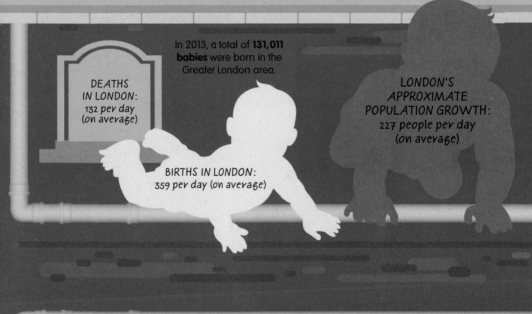

In 2013, a total of **131,011 babies** were born in the Greater London area.

DEATHS IN LONDON:
132 per day
(on average)

LONDON'S APPROXIMATE POPULATION GROWTH:
227 people per day
(on average)

BIRTHS IN LONDON:
359 per day (on average)

... and around **10 PER CENT** more water is used in London than elsewhere in the UK.

Famous Londoners

As you walk around London, you may see some 'Blue Plaques' on buildings, which tell you about the important people who once lived or worked in them. You may not have heard of all of them – but here's a short introduction to some very famous Londoners.

There are lots of places in London named after **Queen Victoria** (1819–1901). She was Britain's monarch when the country was a hugely successful and industrial nation; and at a time when London was the biggest and most populated city on the planet.

KENSINGTON

NOTTING HILL

SOMERS TOWN

WALWORTH

NEWINGTON BUTTS

Rosalind Franklin
(1920–58) was one of the people who helped to reveal the structure of DNA, the stuff that contains genetic information and the 'chemical instructions' for building living things.

Mary Shelley
(1797–1851) finished writing her most famous work, a novel called *Frankenstein*, by the time she was 19 years old. It is the story of a student, Victor Frankenstein, who carries out a scientific experiment to create his own 'Man'.

Charlie Chaplin (1889–1977) was an actor, comedian, writer and director who made many films between 1914 and 1967. In the early part of the 20th century, he was probably the most famous person on the planet.

Michael Faraday (1791–1867) was a scientist who made major discoveries to do with the transformation and generation of electricity, which is now a central part of modern life and technology.

Alfred Hitchcock (1899–1980) wasn't just a great film director, he also developed movie-making techniques and special effects that are still used in films today. He is best known for making exciting 'suspense' and 'thriller' films.

David Beckham (born in 1975) is one of football's most famous faces. He played for his country, England, 115 times (58 of those games as captain). He's also played for club teams all over the world, including Manchester United, Real Madrid, Los Angeles Galaxy, A.C. Milan and Paris Saint-Germain.

LEYTONSTONE

LEYTONSTONE

CITY OF LONDON

LONDON BRIDGE

BRIXTON

Samuel Pepys (1633–1703) always seemed to be around when something important was going on! He witnessed the execution of King Charles I, in 1649, London's Great Plague of 1664–65, the Great Fire of 1666 and England's war with the Dutch (1665–67). His entertaining and detailed diaries tell us a lot of what we know about life in 17th-century London.

David Bowie (1947–2016) was born in Brixton, South London. He went on to become one of the world's most respected and influential music artists.

If you go to Guy's Hospital, near London Bridge Station, you can sit next to a statue of **John Keats** (1795–1821). He trained to be a surgeon at this hospital, but he's better remembered today as one of the most popular of the 19th-century Romantic poets.

Home of Parliament

Britain's decision-makers didn't always meet up in London. In Anglo-Saxon and early Norman times, political meetings took place in other important places – such as Winchester, in the west of England. But in the 12th century, political people started to move into Westminster.

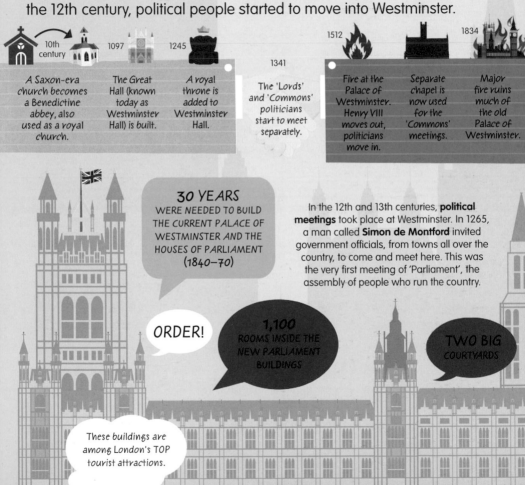

10th century
A Saxon-era church becomes a Benedictine abbey, also used as a royal church.

1097
The Great Hall (known today as Westminster Hall) is built.

1245
A royal throne is added to Westminster Hall.

1341
The 'Lords' and 'Commons' politicians start to meet separately.

1512
Fire at the Palace of Westminster. Henry VIII moves out, politicians move in.

Separate chapel is now used for the 'Commons' meetings.

1834
Major fire ruins much of the old Palace of Westminster.

30 YEARS WERE NEEDED TO BUILD THE CURRENT PALACE OF WESTMINSTER AND THE HOUSES OF PARLIAMENT (1840–70)

In the 12th and 13th centuries, **political meetings** took place at Westminster. In 1265, a man called **Simon de Montford** invited government officials, from towns all over the country, to come and meet here. This was the very first meeting of 'Parliament', the assembly of people who run the country.

ORDER!

1,100 ROOMS INSIDE THE NEW PARLIAMENT BUILDINGS

TWO BIG COURTYARDS

These buildings are among London's TOP tourist attractions.

In 1840–70, Westminster's new government buildings were planned and built in the same 'Gothic' style. Although very grand, the Houses of Parliament are specifically designed for the business of government. They include **two separate chambers** for the 'Lords' and the 'Commons'.

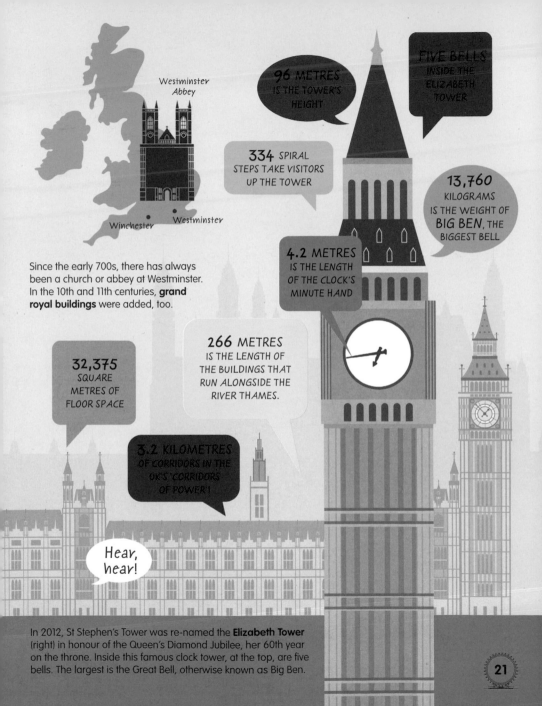

Westminster
Abbey

Winchester   Westminster

96 METRES
IS THE TOWER'S
HEIGHT

FIVE BELLS
INSIDE THE
ELIZABETH
TOWER

334 SPIRAL
STEPS TAKE VISITORS
UP THE TOWER

13,760
KILOGRAMS
IS THE WEIGHT OF
BIG BEN, THE
BIGGEST BELL

4.2 METRES
IS THE LENGTH
OF THE CLOCK'S
MINUTE HAND

Since the early 700s, there has always
been a church or abbey at Westminster.
In the 10th and 11th centuries, **grand
royal buildings** were added, too.

32,375
SQUARE
METRES OF
FLOOR SPACE

266 METRES
IS THE LENGTH OF
THE BUILDINGS THAT
RUN ALONGSIDE THE
RIVER THAMES.

3.2 KILOMETRES
OF CORRIDORS IN THE
UK'S 'CORRIDORS
OF POWER'!

Hear,
hear!

In 2012, St Stephen's Tower was re-named the **Elizabeth Tower**
(right) in honour of the Queen's Diamond Jubilee, her 60th year
on the throne. Inside this famous clock tower, at the top, are five
bells. The largest is the Great Bell, otherwise known as Big Ben.

Buildings from history

Visiting London's older buildings is a great way to explore the history of the city. They are more than just buildings: they represent the many important changes that the city has seen.

Westminster Abbey

12 SEPTEMBER 1940
An unexploded bomb had to be removed from St Paul's Cathedral's roof. If it had gone off, the building would've been destroyed.

9 OCTOBER 1940
Another bomb struck the Cathedral, destroying its 'high altar'.

17 APRIL 1941
An explosion left a hole in the floor, above the crypt.

For Londoners, **St Paul's Cathedral** is an important symbol of the city's strength and survival. The Cathedral was built to replace the one ruined by the Great Fire of 1666, and it has stood firm ever since. It even survived the terrible bombing raids of the Second World War, despite being hit several times.

Edward the Confessor (1003/05–1066)
Henry III (1207–1272)
Edward I (1239–1307)
Edward III (1312–1377)
Richard II (1367–1400)
Henry V (1387–1422)
Edward V (1470–c. 1483)
Henry VII (1457–1509)
Edward VI (1537–1553)
Mary I (1516–1558)
Elizabeth I (1533–1603)
James I (1566–1625)
Charles II (1630–1685)
Mary II (1662–1694)
William III (1650–1702)
Anne (1665–1714)
George II (1683–1760)

Kings and queens have been crowned at **Westminster Abbey** since 1066, when William the Conqueror first came to London. It is also the place where 17 British monarchs have been laid to rest.

MORE THAN **3,300** PEOPLE have been either buried or commemorated at Westminster Abbey.

Built in 1867–71, the **Royal Albert Hall** is one of the best places to see a show in London. It hosts hundreds of performances every year, from classical music concerts to circus shows and tennis matches.

MORE THAN **350** EVENTS take place here each year.

9,999 PIPES are contained in the Hall's permanent musical organ.

↑ **41** METRES in height

83 METRES WIDE

AROUND **5,400** PEOPLE can be seated inside the main arena.

Here's some of the VERY OLDEST STUFF that can be found in London.

3.5 billion years old: fossil imprint of cyanobacteria, on a rock at the Natural History Museum.

2nd century CE: London's oldest place of worship is a Roman temple to the god Mithras, found in Walbrook, City of London.

1075–1101: London's oldest toilets can be found at the north and east walls of the White Tower, Tower of London.

The 'Prime Meridian' line of
longitude runs through the
Greenwich Royal Observatory,
dividing the world into
its Eastern and Western
hemispheres (halves).

The **Royal Observatory** at Greenwich,
in southeast London, was first opened
in 1676. It's where astronomers
mapped the stars and helped to
make scientific improvements to
the way sailors navigated the
globe. It's now a part of the
National Maritime Museum,
which is also at Greenwich.

Western
hemisphere

Eastern
hemisphere

To help with navigation,
the globe was split up
into invisible lines of
'longitude', which run
from the North Pole
to the South Pole.

So – if you visit the Royal
Observatory, you can put one
foot in each hemisphere!

The Monument stands in the City of London,
where Fish Street Hill meets Monument
Street. It was built between 1671 and 1677,
to mark the reconstruction of the city in the
years that followed the Great Fire.

The Monument is 61 metres
high and stands 61 metres from
the exact spot, in Pudding Lane,
where the Great Fire started
on 2 September 1666.

Its designers included a shaft, inside, where
scientific measurements could be made.
There's an underground lab, nearby,
where scientists could keep tabs
on their experiments.

61
METRES

61 METRES

The Monument

1798: Thomas Rule began
to sell food at 34–35
Maiden Lane, Covent
Garden – London's oldest
restaurant address.

Mid-1400s: the city's
oldest timepiece is a
spring-driven clock,
on display at the
British Museum.

Late 16th century: the
building at 41–42 Cloth Fair, in
West Smithfield, is London's
oldest lived-in house.

Tales from the Tower

The majestic Tower of London is one of the city's most famous historical sites. In 1078, William the Conqueror ordered for it to be built as his royal palace and defensive fortress in London.

Value of the jewels: more than £20 BILLION

The Tower of London is where the **Crown Jewels** are kept, under lock and key. They have been stored here since the late 11th century and on public display since the 17th century – except when a king or queen has been using them, of course!

=

200 masterpiece paintings by artists such as Picasso or Monet.

22 TOWERS CAN BE COUNTED AT THE TOWER OF LONDON TODAY

23,500 JEWELS ARE LOCKED UP HERE

AT LEAST SIX RAVENS MUST BE KEPT AT THE TOWER AT ALL TIMES

The oldest part of the Tower of London is the famous **White Tower**, constructed between the late 1070s and 1100. At the time, it was the tallest building in the region, surrounded by 15,000 people living in small wooden homes.

The Tower is famous for its **black ravens**, looked after by the Ravenmaster Yeoman Warder. King Charles II (1630–85) wanted them removed, but he was given this warning: "If the ravens leave the Tower, the kingdom will fall and great harm will come to the nation!"

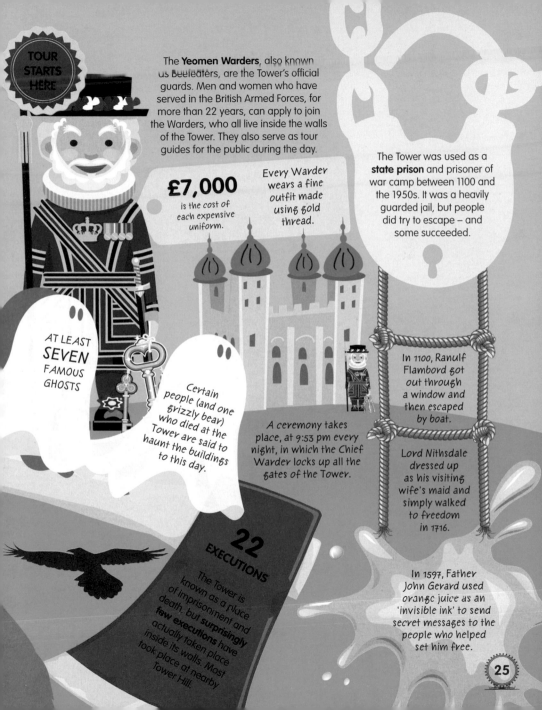

TOUR STARTS HERE

The **Yeomen Warders**, also known as Beefeaters, are the Tower's official guards. Men and women who have served in the British Armed Forces, for more than 22 years, can apply to join the Warders, who all live inside the walls of the Tower. They also serve as tour guides for the public during the day.

£7,000 is the cost of each expensive uniform.

Every Warder wears a fine outfit made using gold thread.

The Tower was used as a **state prison** and prisoner of war camp between 1100 and the 1950s. It was a heavily guarded jail, but people did try to escape – and some succeeded.

AT LEAST **SEVEN** FAMOUS GHOSTS

Certain people (and one grizzly bear) who died at the Tower are said to haunt the buildings to this day.

A ceremony takes place, at 9:53 pm every night, in which the Chief Warder locks up all the gates of the Tower.

In 1100, Ranulf Flambord got out through a window and then escaped by boat.

Lord Nithsdale dressed up as his visiting wife's maid and simply walked to freedom in 1716.

22 EXECUTIONS

The Tower is known as a place of imprisonment and death, but **surprisingly few executions** have actually taken place inside its walls. Most took place at nearby Tower Hill.

In 1597, Father John Gerard used orange juice as an 'invisible ink' to send secret messages to the people who helped set him free.

Modern London

London's modern buildings may not be the tallest in the world, but they are impressive nonetheless. The city is known for its wide variety of architectural styles, with very old structures rubbing shoulders with brand-new ones.

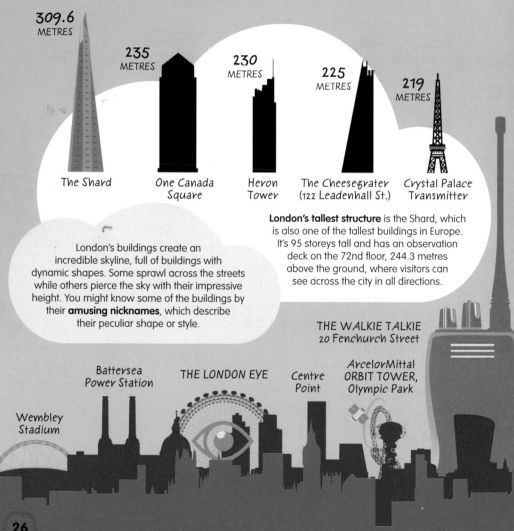

309.6 METRES
The Shard

235 METRES
One Canada Square

230 METRES
Heron Tower

225 METRES
The Cheesegrater (122 Leadenhall St.)

219 METRES
Crystal Palace Transmitter

London's buildings create an incredible skyline, full of buildings with dynamic shapes. Some sprawl across the streets while others pierce the sky with their impressive height. You might know some of the buildings by their **amusing nicknames**, which describe their peculiar shape or style.

London's tallest structure is the Shard, which is also one of the tallest buildings in Europe. It's 95 storeys tall and has an observation deck on the 72nd floor, 244.3 metres above the ground, where visitors can see across the city in all directions.

THE WALKIE TALKIE
20 Fenchurch Street

Wembley Stadium

Battersea Power Station

THE LONDON EYE

Centre Point

ArcelorMittal ORBIT TOWER, Olympic Park

At first glance, some of London's buildings might look like the biggest in the world – but in fact, they are completely dwarfed by those of other cities. The **Burj Khalifa** of Dubai, in the United Arab Emirates, is **more than two-and-a-half times as tall** as the Shard!

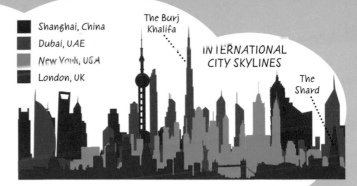

INTERNATIONAL CITY SKYLINES

- Shanghai, China
- Dubai, UAE
- New York, USA
- London, UK

The Burj Khalifa

The Shard

Although it is no longer London's tallest building, the **BT Tower** was the first in the city to be taller than St Paul's Cathedral. Built in 1961–64, it has a revolving restaurant on the 34th floor and lifts that can take you to the very top in just 20 seconds!

34TH FLOOR

7 METRES PER SECOND

Towards the end of construction, a fox was found living on the 72nd floor, feeding on food scraps left by workers.

The Shard was built between March 2009 and July 2012. During the busiest period of building, approximately 1,450 construction workers – from 60 different countries – were involved in the project.

110,000 SQUARE METRES is the Shard's total floor area.

11,000 GLASS PANELS are on its exterior.

44 LIFTS each travel at 6 metres a second.

BT Tower

THE GHERKIN
30 St Mary Axe

THE CHEESEGRATER
122 Leadenhall Street

The Dome
(O₂ Arena)

THE SHARD
Canary Wharf buildings

London's visitors

As the UK's capital city, London receives a HUGE number of visitors every single day, both from overseas and from the rest of the UK. It's an essential destination for anyone who's heard about the sights and sounds of this world-famous city.

APPROXIMATELY **30** MILLION OVERSEAS VISITORS COME TO THE UK (per year)

MORE THAN HALF of the UK's visitors from overseas spend all or part of their holiday in London.

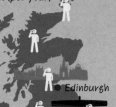

Edinburgh

Belfast

Newcastle

Blackpool

Manchester

Birmingham

Stonehenge   LONDON

In recent times, London has welcomed between 15 million and 18 million overseas tourists every single year. That's on top of the city's many millions of UK-based visitors!

AT LEAST **15** MILLION OVERSEAS VISITORS TO LONDON (per year)

= 1 million tourists

1,884,000 FROM THE USA

1,873,000 FROM FRANCE

1,338,000 FROM GERMANY

1,091,000 FROM ITALY

843,000 FROM SPAIN

So, where do most of these overseas visitors come from? Even though European countries are much closer, people from the **United States of America** make up the biggest group of international tourists each year.

1. BRITISH MUSEUM
2. NATIONAL GALLERY
3. SOUTHBANK CENTRE
4. TATE MODERN
5. NATURAL HISTORY MUSEUM
6. SCIENCE MUSEUM
7. VICTORIA and ALBERT MUSEUM

What makes London such a popular place to visit? Tourists are fond of its many parks and **green spaces**, its free **museums** and **galleries**, the **sporting events**, the historic **buildings** – and events connected with the British **Royal Family**.

Royal weddings and the Queen's birthday

Sporting events, such as the 2012 Olympics

London's 'Theatreland'

★ ★ ★

Free ticket

Perhaps unsurprisingly, the **top seven visitor attractions** in the UK are all in London. Even less surprisingly, these places are all FREE to enter!

World-famous historic buildings

A huge number of parks and other open spaces

From central Europe, London is very easy to get to by train. The **Eurostar services** travel through the Channel Tunnel, which burrows under the English Channel to connect the UK and France.

MORE THAN **10** MILLION PASSENGERS use the Eurostar trains every year.

770 PASSENGERS can be carried by each train – twice as many as a Boeing 747 'Jumbo Jet' can carry.

400 METRES is the length of a Eurostar train.

£24 MILLION is the cost of building each Eurostar train.

229 KPH is the average speed of a Eurostar train.

800 TONNES is the weight of each 18-carriage train.

Shopping!

Visitors to the UK spend more than **£20 BILLION** in the country each year – and more than half of this money gets spent in London. It isn't just the tourist spots that attract all this cash – London is one of the biggest shopping capitals of the world.

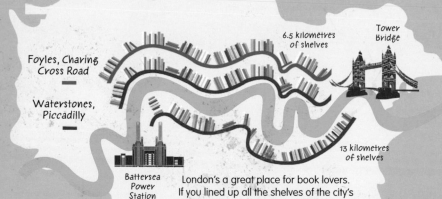

6.5 kilometres of shelves

Tower Bridge

Foyles, Charing Cross Road

Waterstones, Piccadilly

13 kilometres of shelves

Battersea Power Station

London's a great place for book lovers. If you lined up all the shelves of the city's **biggest bookstores**, their books would stretch right along the banks of the River Thames – in between Battersea Power Station and Tower Bridge.

1676
LOCK AND CO. HATTERS
The world's oldest hat store and one of the oldest family businesses on the planet.

1689
EDE AND RAVENSCROFT
The oldest tailor, wig and robe-maker in London (and possibly the world).

1698
BERRY BROTHERS AND RUDD
This is the city's oldest wine-selling business.

1706
TWININGS AND CO.
Thomas Twining bought a coffee house at 216 The Strand, London. Twinings and Co. are now one of the world's most famous tea and coffee suppliers.

LOCK & CO.

EDE & RAVENSCROFT

BERRY BROTHERS & RUDD

TWININGS & CO.

Many of London's **oldest shops and suppliers** are still doing very good business today. Take a stroll along this high street through time …

Harrods started in 1834, as a small grocery shop with just four members of staff in Stepney, East London. It moved to Knightsbridge, West London, in 1849, and now has **330 different departments**.

The Harrods store is lit up at night by up to 12,000 light bulbs. Several hundred of them need to be replaced each day.

100,000 people visit Harrods every day, and up to 300,000 customers visit per day during the Christmas period.

= 300 light bulbs

= 1,000 shoppers

1707 FORTNUM AND MASON
Once a simple grocers, this shop is now a world-famous department store.

1730 FLORIS
This perfume shop, at 89 Jermyn Street, is still being run by descendants of the original owners.

1750 SWAINE ADENEY BRIGG
Makers of fine leather goods, hats and umbrellas.

1760 HAMLEYS
The world's oldest toy store, which sells more than 50,000 different toys and games.

1797 HATCHARD'S
The UK's oldest bookstore, which still exists at Piccadilly, where the company first started out.

FORTNUM & MASON

FLORIS

SWAINE ADENEY BRIGG

HAMLEYS

HATCHARD'S

Hamleys opened in 1760 and moved to Regent Street in 1881. Inside, you can explore its **seven floors** and **5,000 square metres** of playing space!

Museums and galleries

London's museums and art galleries are among the most-visited places in the capital. Many of them are free to enter and house millions of objects and artworks that you can get close to – or even touch.

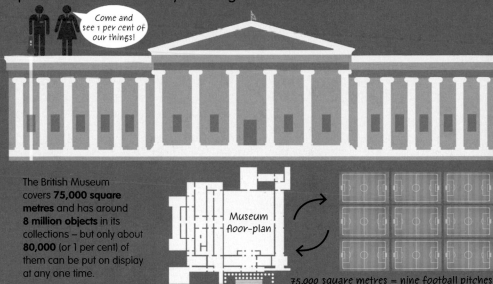

Come and see 1 per cent of our things!

The British Museum covers **75,000 square metres** and has around **8 million objects** in its collections – but only about **80,000 (or 1 per cent)** of them can be put on display at any one time.

Museum floor-plan

75,000 square metres = nine football pitches

London's Natural History Museum is home to an astonishing **80 MILLION** specimens from all over the planet. The coloured windows below help to show the size of each of the museum's collections.

More than 34 million insect and arachnid specimens

More than 29 million other animal specimens

More than 7 million vertebrate, invertebrate and plant fossils

More than 6 million botanical (plant-related) specimens

More than 1.5 million books, artworks and other documents

More than 500,000 rocks, gems and minerals

The galleries in the Museum of London represent **450,000 years** of the city's history … they also contain a few surprising and unusual items.

| Roman bikini bottoms: from 1st century CE | Ice skates: from the 12th century | Baby clothes of Queen Victoria's children: 1840s | Queen Victoria's knickers: mid-19th century | Corset worn by a female French trapeze artist: 1860s | Mechanical automaton (a human-like machine): 1870s | A 'Mickey Mouse' children's gas mask: c. late 1930s |

The Victoria and Albert Museum, in Kensington, was opened in 1852. It contains **145 galleries** displaying more than **6.5 million cultural objects and artefacts** from Europe, North America, Asia and northern Africa. The items span **5,000 years** of art and architecture. There are:

202,500 paintings and drawings

28,000 fashion and jewellery items

2,050,000 architecture items

160,000 Asian objects

20,000 childhood objects

74,000 ceramics

1,905,000 theatrical objects

17,500 sculptures

38,000 textiles items

1.5 million prints and books

14,000 furniture items

31,000 metalwork items

500,000 photography items

6,000 glassware items

MOST POPULAR
Which London museums attract the most visitors each year?

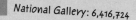 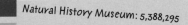

British Museum: 6,695,213

National Gallery: 6,416,724

Tate Modern (art gallery): 5,785,427

Natural History Museum: 5,388,295

Science Museum: 3,356,072

33

Royal city

The United Kingdom is a nation with a monarchy, which means it has a king or queen as its Head of State. Buckingham Palace is the monarch's main home and place of work in London. Since 1837, four kings and two queens have lived there.

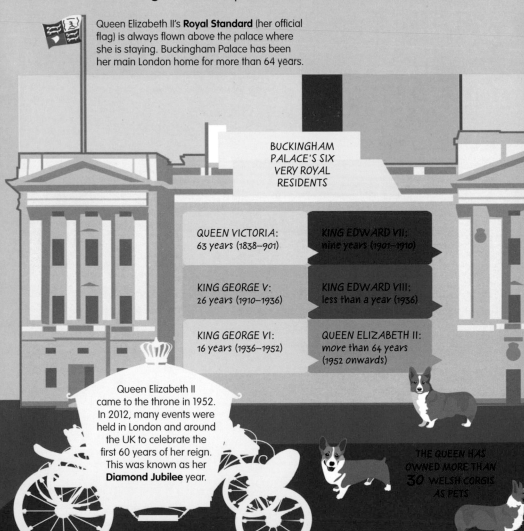

Queen Elizabeth II's **Royal Standard** (her official flag) is always flown above the palace where she is staying. Buckingham Palace has been her main London home for more than 64 years.

BUCKINGHAM PALACE'S SIX VERY ROYAL RESIDENTS

QUEEN VICTORIA: 63 years (1838–901)

KING EDWARD VII: nine years (1901–1910)

KING GEORGE V: 26 years (1910–1936)

KING EDWARD VIII: less than a year (1936)

KING GEORGE VI: 16 years (1936–1952)

QUEEN ELIZABETH II: more than 64 years (1952 onwards)

Queen Elizabeth II came to the throne in 1952. In 2012, many events were held in London and around the UK to celebrate the first 60 years of her reign. This was known as her **Diamond Jubilee** year.

THE QUEEN HAS OWNED MORE THAN 30 WELSH CORGIS AS PETS

41
CANNONS ARE FIRED IN HONOUR OF THE QUEEN'S BIRTHDAY

MORE THAN **1,000** ARMY TROOPS AND OFFICERS TAKE PART IN THE TROOPING THE COLOUR PARADES

400 MUSICIANS PERFORM AS PART OF THE MILITARY MARCHES

Queen Elizabeth II was born on 21 April 1926 – but her birthday is officially marked by a ceremony called **Trooping the Colour**, which is always held on a Saturday in June.

Buckingham Palace has 19 State rooms, 52 Royal and guest bedrooms, 188 staff bedrooms, 92 offices and **78 bathrooms**.

More than **800 members of staff** work at the Palace.

Wow! There are about **775 rooms** in here!

The **Queen's Guards** are on duty for two hours at a time. As each second passes, they must remain totally alert.

There are 1,514 doors, 760 windows, and more than **40,000 light bulbs** in the Palace.

From basement to roof, the total floor area of the Palace is **77,000 square metres**.

More than **50,000 people** visit the Palace each year. The kitchen can serve a sit-down meal to up to **600 people** at a time.

NO RESTING

NO SLEEPING

NO SMOKING

NO EATING

Kensington Palace was once the London home of William and Kate, the Duke and Duchess of Cambridge.

St James's Palace is London's 'ceremonial' Royal residence.

Transport in London

London is one of the largest, busiest capital cities on the planet. Millions of people use London's incredible transport networks to travel in, out, across and around the city each day.

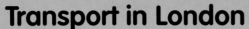

Approximately **139 MILLION people** travel through London's airports every year. That's more than twice the total population of the UK.

✈ → DEPARTURES

London's biggest, busiest airport is Heathrow. Every day, an average of **201,000 people** pass through its large terminals on business trips, holidays, or to transfer to another flight.

TAKE-OFFS AND LANDINGS AT LONDON'S AIRPORTS (PER DAY): 2,700

ANNUAL PASSENGERS AT HEATHROW: 73 MILLION
BUSINESS PASSENGERS (PER YEAR): 22 MILLION (30%)
LEISURE PASSENGERS (PER YEAR): 51 MILLION (70%)

AVERAGE TIME BETWEEN EACH TAKE-OFF AND LANDING AT HEATHROW: 45 SECONDS

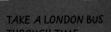

TAKE A LONDON BUS THROUGH TIME ...

1829
The first London bus service ran between Paddington and Bank stations. Each bus was pulled by three horses and carried up to 22 passengers.

1907
Up until 1907, London bus routes all had a different colour.

1914
During the First World War, buses transported the 'carrier pigeons' used to send vital messages over long distances.

Around **7,500 buses** carry more than **6 million people** around Greater London every weekday. That's an average of **800 people** using each bus each day.

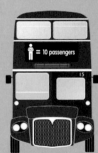

= 10 passengers

LOST PROPERTY!

These are the **top five** most common items left behind on London's massive transport network each year.

KEYS: 10,000

MOBILE PHONES: 20,000

UMBRELLAS: 11,000

MONEY WALLETS: 11,500

TRAVELCARD WALLETS: 18,000

Roughly **60,000 city streets**

About **20,000 landmarks**

Black cabs have a tall, rounded shape. Originally, this was to make room for men's top hats, popular from the 18th century to mid-20th century.

Among London's taxis are the famous **black cabs**. Their drivers spend up to four years learning **The Knowledge**, which involves memorizing loads of different routes and locations in London.

A to Z

There are more than 19,000 black cabs in London.

The Tube network

First opened in 1863, London's famous 'Tube' network is a very popular way to get around the city – underground. Each year, approximately **1.3 billion people** take trips on the Tube.

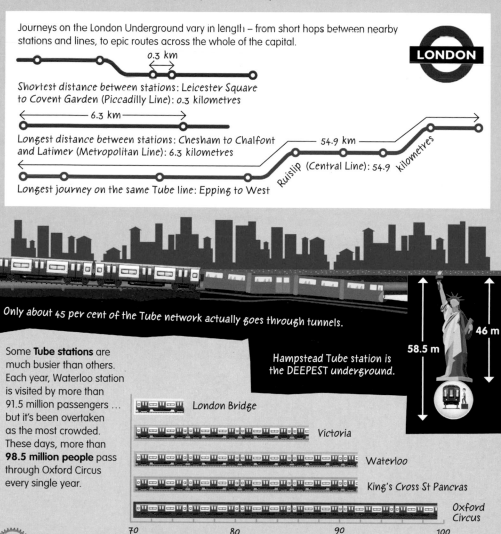

Journeys on the London Underground vary in length – from short hops between nearby stations and lines, to epic routes across the whole of the capital.

LONDON

0.3 km

Shortest distance between stations: Leicester Square to Covent Garden (Piccadilly Line): 0.3 kilometres

6.3 km

Longest distance between stations: Chesham to Chalfont and Latimer (Metropolitan Line): 6.3 kilometres

54.9 km

Ruislip (Central Line): 54.9 kilometres

Longest journey on the same Tube line: Epping to West

Only about 45 per cent of the Tube network actually goes through tunnels.

Some **Tube stations** are much busier than others. Each year, Waterloo station is visited by more than 91.5 million passengers … but it's been overtaken as the most crowded. These days, more than **98.5 million people** pass through Oxford Circus every single year.

Hampstead Tube station is the DEEPEST underground.

58.5 m

46 m

London Bridge

Victoria

Waterloo

King's Cross St Pancras

Oxford Circus

70   80   90   100

Passengers per year (in millions)

If you could unravel all the London Underground **rail lines** and lay them end to end, you could take a train up to Blackpool for a nice holiday by the seaside!

In one year, London's Tube trains travel more than 76 million kilometres. That's about half the distance between the Earth and Sun!

Blackpool

400 km

London

As the Underground and Overground networks are extended, new stations are being opened in London as time goes by. But there are also some that are **no longer used**. Most are still there, under the streets … either forgotten about or used to film scenes in movies!

ABANDONED!

CLOSED!

DOWN AND OUT!

NO ENTRY!

DON'T STOP HERE!

REPLACED

NOT IN USE

1900:
King William
Street

1930s:
British Museum
station

1932:
Down
Street

1934:
Brompton
Road

1939:
Lord's

1947:
Wood Lane

1994:
Aldwych

Travelling by Tube would be a much more tiring business if we didn't have all the escalators!

MOST escalators: 23, at Waterloo Tube station

LONGEST escalator: 60 metres, at Angel Tube station

Just ONE escalator at the Angel Tube station can take you quite far underground …

SHORTEST escalator: 4.1 metres, at Stratford Tube station

Stories from the streets

In the story of Dick Whittington, he went to London because he'd heard that the city's streets were 'paved with gold'. Of course, this isn't actually true, but the streets of London are certainly full of history – and sometimes mystery.

A is for ARTILLERY LANE, E1

B is for BLEEDING HEART YARD, EC1

Many of London's streets take their name from something associated with that part of the city. Historians and language experts have explained the meanings behind some names. Others have been harder to unravel.

PICCADILLY:
Probably owes its name to small pieces of material, called 'pickadils', used to make clothes here in Tudor times (1485–1603).

PALL MALL:
Named after a 17th-century 'ball and mallet' game, similar to croquet, that was played in nearby St James's Park.

SOHO SQUARE:
The Soho area was once open fields. It may be named after a hunting cry. Hunters would shout 'So-Ho!' if they spotted a hare to chase.

Thorney Island

The famous door to NUMBER 10 DOWNING STREET cannot be opened from the outside. It has no handle.

C is for CYCLOPS MEWS, E14

D is for DOG KENNEL HILL, SE22

POULTRY:
This short street gets its name from the medieval 'poulterers' markets', where chickens, geese, turkeys and ducks were bought and sold.

Downing Street used to be known as **Thorney Island**, because two branches of the River Tyburn flowed around this location in medieval times. It is now the official residence of the prime minister, and is one of the UK's most heavily guarded addresses.

Since 1924, 10 Downing Street has had a CHIEF MOUSER – a cat for catching mice.

F is for FRYING PAN ALLEY, E1

H is for HA HA ROAD, SE18

J is for JUPITER WAY, N7

500,000 PEOPLE visit OXFORD STREET each day. It's Europe's busiest shopping street.

OXFORD ST. W1
CITY OF WESTMINSTER

K is for KITE YARD, SW11

2.4 KILOMETRES is the total length of Oxford Street. Approximately **300** SHOPS are on this single stretch of road.

Q is for QUILL LANE, SW15

R is for RABBIT ROW, W8

If you walk down Cannon Street, in the City of London, you may come across the London Stone. Now just half a metre tall, this stone once sat at the very centre of Londinium, the Roman trading town.

Londinium

T is for TWEEZER'S ALLEY, WC2

U is for UPHILL DRIVE, NW7

V is for VINEGAR YARD, SE1

The London Stone may have been a 'milestone', used to measure distances between Roman London and other places across Britain.

Y is for YULETIDE CLOSE, NW10

Some London addresses have been made famous in books and films, as places lived in or visited by their characters.

MY FAIR LADY

221B BAKER STREET: The home of a detective called SHERLOCK HOLMES in the stories written by Sir Arthur Conan Doyle.

347 PICCADILLY: A fictional mansion, rented by a London visitor called Count De Ville, who turns out to be a vampire – named COUNT DRACULA – in a novel by Bram Stoker.

27A WIMPOLE STREET: The address of Henry Higgins in a play about a Covent Garden flower seller, ELIZA DOOLITTLE. The play was later turned into a film and musical called MY FAIR LADY.

JACK COLLET (hanged for his crimes in 1691): To fool rich travellers, he carried out many of his robberies while dressed up in the robes of a bishop.

TOM ROWLAND (executed in 1699): This cheeky criminal used to dress up as a woman, so that his victims wouldn't suspect he was about to rob them.

NATHANIEL HAWES (c. 1701–21): A highwayman who was finally caught by one of his own victims, who managed to get hold of Hawes's pistol during an attempted robbery.

In the 17th and 18th centuries, different parts of London were linked by long highways, used by wealthy travellers with horse-drawn carriages. These carriages were sometimes ambushed by armed 'robbers of the roads', known as **highwaymen**.

Z is for ZENITH LODGE, N3

The River Thames

Why were so many cities and settlements built next to rivers? The rivers provided a fresh water supply, a natural defence, and a way of carrying goods in and out by boat. This is why London grew up along the Thames.

The Thames is **the second-longest river** in the UK, after the Severn. It flows through many towns and cities on its course to the North Sea.

Wildlife observers and conservationists have spotted a **wide variety of animals** in the Thames, including a rare type of seahorse – found at Greenwich in 2012 – and a whale that swam into Central London in 2006!

THE *CUTTY SARK*: A ship that brought tea from China in 1869–77, which has been moored in Greenwich since the 1950s.

46 WILDLIFE CONSERVATION (PROTECTION) CENTRES

350 INVERTEBRATE SPECIES ON OR NEAR THE RIVERBED

125 SPECIES OF FISH, POSSIBLY MORE

HMS BELFAST: Once a military cruiser, built in 1936–38, it's now a naval museum that opened to the public in 1971.

The Fleet: DRIVEN UNDERGROUND IN THE 18TH CENTURY

The Tyburn: DISAPPEARED UNDER WESTMINSTER

The Walbrook: ONCE DIVIDED ROMAN LONDON IN TWO

The Effra: STILL FLOWING UNDER SOUTH LONDON

non-tidal Thames: 68%

tidal: 32%

Parts of the Thames with high and low tides

As London has grown bigger and bigger, some of its rivers have either disappeared or been forced underground by construction.

The **Thames Barrier** is a futuristic-looking defence system. It has **ten huge gates**. The gates can be raised to protect Central London from being flooded by extremely high tides or storm surges heading up from the North Sea.

125 SQUARE KILOMETRES IS THE AREA OF CENTRAL LONDON THAT THE BARRIER PROTECTS

520 METRES IS THE WIDTH OF THE BARRIER

15 METRES IS THE HEIGHT OF EACH RAISED GATE

3.3 MILLION KILOGRAMS IS THE WEIGHT OF ONE GATE

1982 IS THE YEAR OF ITS FIRST OPERATION

175 USES SINCE ITS CONSTRUCTION

HQS *WELLINGTON*: A former Royal Navy ship, first put to sea in 1934.

THE *GOLDEN HINDE II*: A replica (built in 1973) of the ship that Sir Francis Drake sailed around the world in, from 1577–80.

TS *QUEEN MARY*: Built in 1933, this steam ferry is now a floating restaurant.

flows through 16 major towns

214 bridges

60 active shipping terminals

more than 200 rowing clubs

190 islands

LENGTH: 346 km

WIDEST POINT 29 km

17 tunnels pass through it

Other mammals

More than 60 per cent of the mammals spotted in the Thames are species of seals.

43

London's bridges

The Millennium Bridge

There are more than 30 rail, road and footbridges across the Thames river, between west London and the North Sea. When you walk over the capital's crossings, you're also stepping through its history.

The first bridge on this site was opened in 1816. It was the very first London bridge to be built out of iron.

When a bridge was first opened here, in 1750, dogs were banned from crossing, and vandals were warned that they would be executed if they drew graffiti on it!

Vauxhall Bridge

Westminster Bridge

Chelsea Bridge

Waterloo Bridge

Waterloo Bridge was built using Portland stone, a kind of limestone. The chemical make-up of the stone means that it actually 'cleans itself' when it reacts with the London rainwater.

When the site of this crossing was first dug up, weapons and human bones were found. A battle probably took place here between ancient Britons and the invading Romans (see page 6).

Waterloo Bridge was built by female construction workers during the Second World War.

LONDON BRIDGE: A BRIDGE THROUGH TIME

The city's first bridge across the Thames was built by the Romans, in around CE 50. It was made out of wood.

The first-ever stone version of the bridge was built in the medieval period, in 1176–1209.

CITY ON THE THAMES

TIMBER BRIDGES

FIRST STONE CROSSING

Between 1201 and the 1750s the bridge was covered in houses and shops.

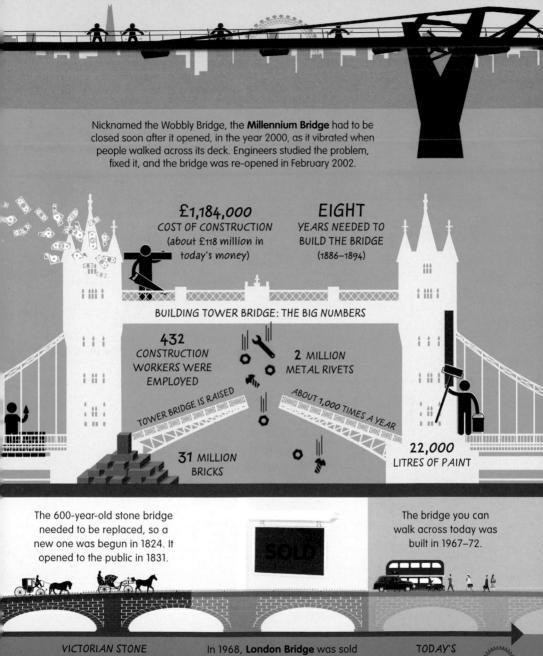

Nicknamed the Wobbly Bridge, the **Millennium Bridge** had to be closed soon after it opened, in the year 2000, as it vibrated when people walked across its deck. Engineers studied the problem, fixed it, and the bridge was re-opened in February 2002.

£1,184,000
COST OF CONSTRUCTION
(about £118 million in today's money)

EIGHT
YEARS NEEDED TO BUILD THE BRIDGE
(1886–1894)

BUILDING TOWER BRIDGE: THE BIG NUMBERS

432
CONSTRUCTION WORKERS WERE EMPLOYED

2 MILLION
METAL RIVETS

TOWER BRIDGE IS RAISED

ABOUT 1,000 TIMES A YEAR

31 MILLION BRICKS

22,000
LITRES OF PAINT

The 600-year-old stone bridge needed to be replaced, so a new one was begun in 1824. It opened to the public in 1831.

SOLD

The bridge you can walk across today was built in 1967–72.

VICTORIAN STONE ARCH BRIDGE

In 1968, **London Bridge** was sold to an American businessman for $2.46 million (about £1.65 million).

TODAY'S CROSSING

Wildlife in the city

Britain emerged from the last ice age about 11,500 years ago. As the ice sheets got smaller, and the temperatures rose, grasslands and woodlands developed around the London region. Smaller parts of these habitats still survive today.

By the time human beings started settling in the area we now call London, there would've been aurochs, elk and deer running around its vast, **ancient woodlands**.

SOME OF LONDON'S
MOST ANCIENT WOODLANDS

1. Cherry Tree Wood, East Finchley
2. Coldfall Wood, Muswell Hill • 3. Epping Forest
4. The Great North Wood • 5. Highgate Wood
6. Oak Hill Wood, East Barnet • 7. Old Park Wood, Harefield • 8. Oxleas Wood, Greenwich
9. Queen's Wood, Haringey • 10. Scratchwood, Mill Hill • 11. Sydenham Hill Wood
12. Wimbledon Common

10.

6.

1.

7.

3.

2.

Deer

5. 9.

Stag
(male deer)

8.

12. Auroch
(wild ox)

4.

11.

Elk

PEREGRINE FALCONS
returned to London and began breeding at the top of tall buildings in the early 2000s.

The **ring-tailed parakeet** is the only species of parrot that lives in the UK, in the wild. They started to breed in Kent and southeast London in around 1969, and now there are many thousands of them! Some birds of prey have also returned to London after many years.

RED KITES
started to return to London in around 2005.

There are more than **30,000** parakeets in London and Southeast England.

258,000 foxes live in Britain ...

33,000 of them live in towns and cities.

Workers digging around at London's many construction sites sometimes find the remains of large animals, including beasts that have been **extinct in Britain** for thousands of years.

1. Crocodile bones, from Islington

2. Walrus, hippo, rhino, and mammoth remains, Fitzrovia

3. Lion remains, Charing Cross

4. Hippopotamus bones, Trafalgar Square

5. Elephant bones, Whitehall

6. Brown bear bones, Woolwich

7. Mammoth and walrus bones, King's Cross

AT LEAST **200** WATER VOLES AT THE WETLAND CENTRE

Before the 1990s, **water voles** lived in many wetland habitats in and around Greater London. They have now disappeared from most of these locations. In recent years, conservationists have been trying to protect these animals and their habitats. The **London Wetland Centre** in Barnes, Southwest London, now provides a natural home for water voles.

That's roughly **1,000** beetles for every ONE human in the city. Aargh!

10,000 FOXES LIVE IN LONDON

THAT'S **4** PER CENT OF BRITAIN'S FOX POPULATION

People sometimes say that there are more rats than there are people in London, but this is far from the truth. You're much more likely to find lots of **urban beetles** crawling in and around the homes of Londoners!

There are about **20,000** times more beetles than rats in London.

RATS VS. BEETLES

Parks and zoos

London is a bustling city, but it's also full of green spaces – parks and gardens that sit amongst the busy streets and towering buildings, where people can meet, relax, play or take a break from work.

The biggest parks in Central and Greater London are the **eight Royal Parks**, which are normally free to enter and wander around. At various times of the year, concerts and special events take place in these parks.

Added together, the Royal Parks and Gardens make up approximately **20 square kilometres** of green space. However, that's nothing compared to the overall size of Greater London, which sprawls across an incredible 1,572 square kilometres!

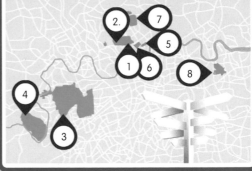

1. **HYDE PARK:** 1.4 square kilometres

2. **KENSINGTON GARDENS:** 0.98 square kilometres

3. **RICHMOND PARK:** 9.55 square kilometres

4. **BUSHY PARK:** 4.45 square kilometres

5. **ST JAMES'S PARK:** 0.23 square kilometres

6. **THE GREEN PARK:** 0.16 square kilometres

7. **REGENT'S PARK and PRIMROSE HILL:** 1.59 square kilometres

8. **GREENWICH PARK:** 0.73 square kilometres

The Hyde Park Winter Wonderland takes place each year, from November to January.

The Open Air Theatre, Regent's Park

London's parks aren't just for wandering around with an ice cream. You can go to **concerts and sporting events** in the parks – and Regent's Park also has its own Open Air Theatre for plays, musicals and other shows.

A summer music festival in Hyde Park

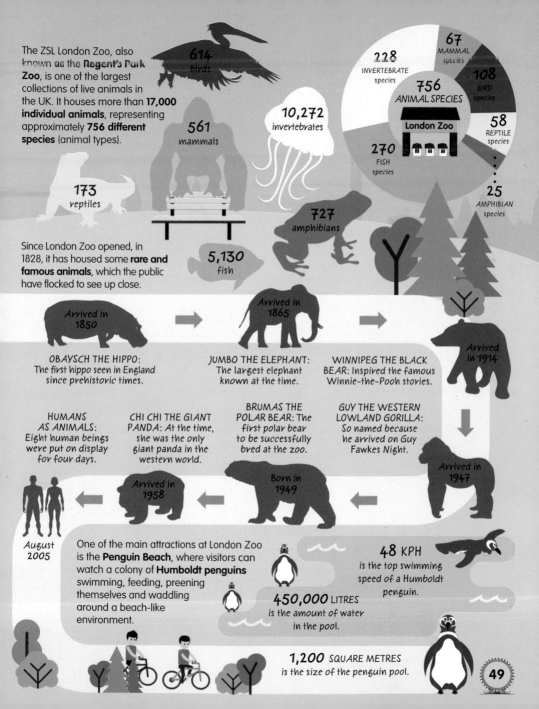

The ZSL London Zoo, also known as the **Regent's Park Zoo**, is one of the largest collections of live animals in the UK. It houses more than **17,000 individual animals**, representing approximately **756 different species** (animal types).

614 birds

561 mammals

10,272 invertebrates

173 reptiles

228 INVERTEBRATE species

67 MAMMAL species

756 ANIMAL SPECIES

London Zoo

108 BIRD species

58 REPTILE species

270 FISH species

25 AMPHIBIAN species

Since London Zoo opened, in 1828, it has housed some **rare and famous animals**, which the public have flocked to see up close.

727 amphibians

5,130 fish

Arrived in 1850

Arrived in 1865

Arrived in 1914

OBAYSCH THE HIPPO: The first hippo seen in England since prehistoric times.

JUMBO THE ELEPHANT: The largest elephant known at the time.

WINNIPEG THE BLACK BEAR: Inspired the famous Winnie-the-Pooh stories.

HUMANS AS ANIMALS: Eight human beings were put on display for four days.

CHI CHI THE GIANT PANDA: At the time, she was the only giant panda in the western world.

BRUMAS THE POLAR BEAR: The first polar bear to be successfully bred at the zoo.

GUY THE WESTERN LOWLAND GORILLA: So named because he arrived on Guy Fawkes Night.

Arrived in 1958

Born in 1949

Arrived in 1947

August 2005

One of the main attractions at London Zoo is the **Penguin Beach**, where visitors can watch a colony of **Humboldt penguins** swimming, feeding, preening themselves and waddling around a beach-like environment.

48 KPH is the top swimming speed of a Humboldt penguin.

450,000 LITRES is the amount of water in the pool.

1,200 SQUARE METRES is the size of the penguin pool.

49

Active city

If you look beyond the cars, buses and trains in the capital, you'll see that there are plenty of people trying to stay fit and active. The city is also home some world-famous sporting events.

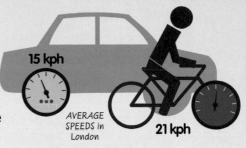

15 kph

AVERAGE SPEEDS in London

21 kph

Because of all the traffic lights and congestion, the **average speed of a car** in London is just 15 kph. This is why it can be much speedier to get around the city by bike!

610,000
CYCLING JOURNEYS are made in London every day.

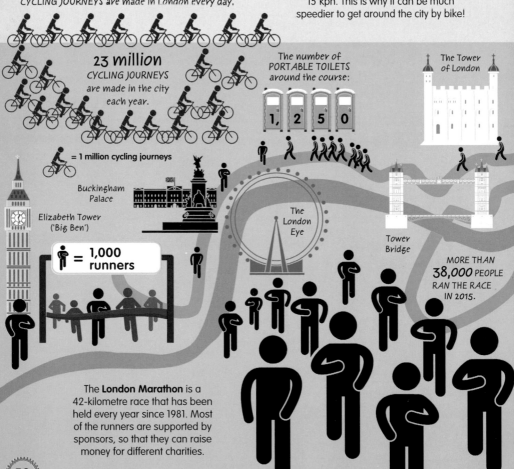

23 million CYCLING JOURNEYS are made in the city each year.

= 1 million cycling journeys

The number of PORTABLE TOILETS around the course:

1, 2 5 0

The Tower of London

Buckingham Palace

Elizabeth Tower ('Big Ben')

The London Eye

Tower Bridge

= **1,000 runners**

MORE THAN **38,000** PEOPLE RAN THE RACE IN 2015.

The **London Marathon** is a 42-kilometre race that has been held every year since 1981. Most of the runners are supported by sponsors, so that they can raise money for different charities.

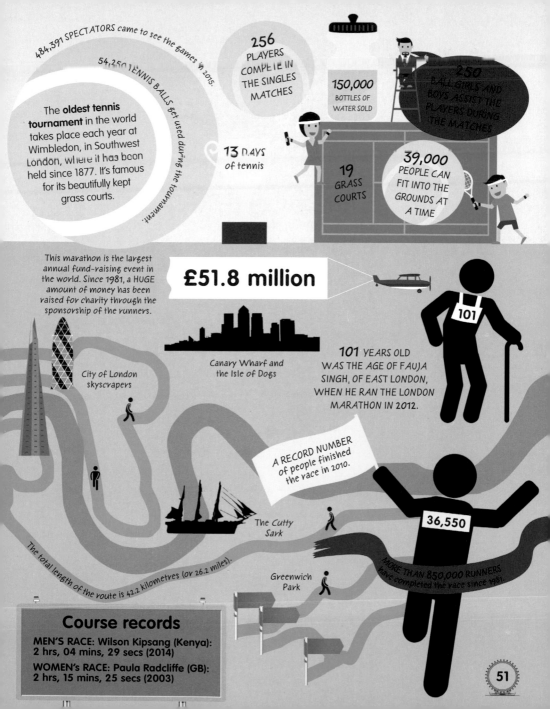

484,391 SPECTATORS came to see the games in 2015.

54,250 TENNIS BALLS get used during the tournament.

256 PLAYERS COMPETE IN THE SINGLES MATCHES

150,000 BOTTLES OF WATER SOLD

250 BALL GIRLS AND BOYS ASSIST THE PLAYERS DURING THE MATCHES

The **oldest tennis tournament** in the world takes place each year at Wimbledon, in Southwest London, where it has been held since 1877. It's famous for its beautifully kept grass courts.

13 DAYS of tennis

19 GRASS COURTS

39,000 PEOPLE CAN FIT INTO THE GROUNDS AT A TIME

This marathon is the largest annual fund-raising event in the world. Since 1981, a HUGE amount of money has been raised for charity through the sponsorship of the runners.

£51.8 million

City of London skyscrapers

Canary Wharf and the Isle of Dogs

101

101 YEARS OLD WAS THE AGE OF FAUJA SINGH, OF EAST LONDON, WHEN HE RAN THE LONDON MARATHON IN 2012.

A RECORD NUMBER of people finished the race in 2010.

The total length of the route is 42.2 kilometres (or 26.2 miles).

The *Cutty Sark*

Greenwich Park

36,550

MORE THAN 850,000 RUNNERS have completed the race since 1981.

Course records
MEN'S RACE: Wilson Kipsang (Kenya): 2 hrs, 04 mins, 29 secs (2014)
WOMEN's RACE: Paula Radcliffe (GB): 2 hrs, 15 mins, 25 secs (2003)

Olympic London

London has a great sporting history, and it's been the host city for the Summer Olympic Games three times – in 1908, 1948 and 2012. In 2012, the competitions took place all over the capital, as well as at its purpose-built Olympic Park.

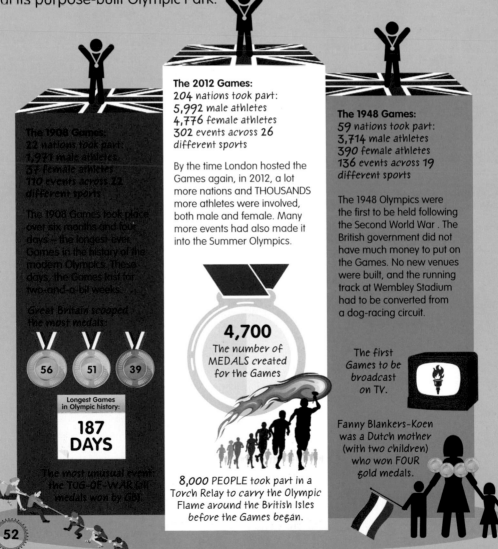

The 2012 Games:
204 nations took part:
5,992 male athletes
4,776 female athletes
302 events across 26 different sports

By the time London hosted the Games again, in 2012, a lot more nations and THOUSANDS more athletes were involved, both male and female. Many more events had also made it into the Summer Olympics.

4,700
The number of MEDALS created for the Games

8,000 PEOPLE took part in a Torch Relay to carry the Olympic Flame around the British Isles before the Games began.

The 1908 Games:
22 nations took part:
1,971 male athletes
37 female athletes
110 events across 22 different sports

The 1908 Games took place over six months and four days – the longest-ever Games in the history of the modern Olympics. These days, the Games last for two-and-a-half weeks.

Great Britain scooped the most medals:

56 | 51 | 39

Longest Games in Olympic history:
187 DAYS

The most unusual event: the TUG-OF-WAR all medals won by GBT.

The 1948 Games:
59 nations took part:
3,714 male athletes
390 female athletes
136 events across 19 different sports

The 1948 Olympics were the first to be held following the Second World War . The British government did not have much money to put on the Games. No new venues were built, and the running track at Wembley Stadium had to be converted from a dog-racing circuit.

The first Games to be broadcast on TV.

Fanny Blankers-Koen was a Dutch mother (with two children) who won FOUR gold medals.

To build the **London 2012 Olympic Zone**, a huge area of industrial wasteland in East London was cleaned up and cleared. This made way for six new sporting arenas and a BMX racetrack – as well as thousands of newly planted trees and plants.

Number of venues in the main zone:

7

4,000 trees were planted in the new Olympic Park

2 million square metres of ground is covered by the Olympic Park.

2,000 newts were moved to new homes during the Park's construction.

During the London 2012 Games, **32 new world records** were set, across eight different sports. Eight of the records were achieved in swimming – and China, Great Britain and the USA each managed to set **five world records** each.

£5.3 billion The estimated TOTAL COST of building all the new venues.

3

LONDON has hosted the Summer Olympic Games a record number of times.

22

MICHAEL PHELPS has more Olympic medals than any other athlete.

8

Jacqueline Freney (of Australia) won EIGHT Paralympic gold medals in the swimming pool.

THE PARALYMPICS

The **London 2012 Paralympics** was the 14th Summer Paralympics for athletes with disabilities. When London hosted the Olympics in 1948, the UK's Stoke Mandeville Games were also held – for athletes who had been disabled by fighting in the Second World War. The first 'official' Paralympic Games were held in Rome, in 1960.

The 2012 Games:
164 nations took part
4,302 athletes
503 events across 20 different sports

53

1314
Some form of football has been played in London since 1314, when the game was first created.

1409
King Henry IV of England banned the game – possibly because it was too violent.

1581
Smaller teams, set positions on the pitch and referees were created.

1860
Cray Wanderers FC founded – the oldest Greater London football club that still exists.

1863
Rules for the modern game of football were written down in London.

The biggest London teams all play on superb pitches inside **modern stadiums**. But which venues can seat the most spectators..?

Soccer city

Football is the most popular sport in the UK, so it'll come as no surprise to hear that London is jam-packed with soccer fans. It's also home to some of the biggest and most successful teams in Britain.

In the Greater London area, there are **14 professional** and **more than 80 non-professional football teams**. At the professional clubs, the players and coaching staff all earn their living through football.

GREATER LONDON'S PRO FOOTBALL CLUBS

14 Wimbledon
13 West Ham United
2 Barnet
1 Arsenal
2 Tottenham
3 Brentford
4 Charlton Athletic
12 Leyton
9 Dagenham and Redbridge
12 Tottenham Hotspur
White City (Queens Park Rangers)
1 Holloway (Arsenal)
13 West Ham
5 Chelsea
11 Queens Park Rangers
3 Brentford
8 Fulham
5 Chelsea
10 Millwall
4 Charlton
14 Wimbledon
6 Crystal Palace
10 Leyton Orient
8 Fulham
7 Dagenham & Redbridge
6 Crystal Palace

38 GAMES UNBEATEN (2003/04 season)

12 FA CUP TITLES

13 ENGLISH LEAGUE TITLES

Arsenal were the first London team to be English League Champions, in 1931. They've **won the FA Cup** more times than any other club. In 2003/04, they were **unbeaten in all 38 games** of the domestic league season.

Arsenal FC

54

60,338 SEATS AT THE EMIRATES STADIUM (ARSENAL FC)

41,798 SEATS AT STAMFORD BRIDGE (CHELSEA FC)

36,230 SEATS AT WHITE HART LANE (TOTTENHAM HOTSPUR FC)

Timeline

1870s
London's Royal Engineers AFC developed the 'passing style' of football.

1872
The first FA Cup Final was held, at London's Kennington Oval ground.

1879
Fulham FC founded – the oldest London club still playing in a pro' league.

1882
The London Football Association was set up.

1891
Woolwich Arsenal became London's first-ever professional team. The club moved to North London in 1913 and is now known as Arsenal FC.

When football was first played, **there weren't many rules**, it was rough and rowdy and there were irregular numbers of players in the teams. It wasn't until 1863, at a meeting in a London tavern, that the rules were properly sorted out.

The FA Cup is the **oldest annual football competition** in the world, first held in the 1871/72 season. **More than 700** English and Welsh teams enter the knock-out competition each year.

ARSENAL: **12** wins

TOTTENHAM HOTSPUR: **8** wins

CHELSEA: **7** wins

WANDERERS FC: **5** wins

WEST HAM UNITED: **3** wins

CHARLTON ATHLETIC: **1** win

CRYSTAL PALACE: **1** win

WIMBLEDON FC: **1** win

38 FA CUP FINAL WINS FOR LONDON CLUBS

1971: UEFA CUP WINNERS' CUP CHAMPIONS

2012: UEFA CHAMPIONS LEAGUE WINNERS

2013: UEFA EUROPA LEAGUE WINNERS

Chelsea are the most successful London team in European club competitions. In 2012, they became the **first and only London team** to win the UEFA Champions League. They are also the **only British team** to have won all three UEFA club competitions.

Chelsea FC

400 MILLION FANS
CHELSEA FC

100 MILLION FANS
ARSENAL FC

11 MILLION FANS
TOTTENHAM HOTSPUR FC

Hidden London

Walking around London, you can see that it's full of grand buildings and amazing landmarks. But there also many things that you cannot see – secret places underground and some incredible structures that were planned but never built.

Watkin's Tower (1890s)

Designed to be 45 metres taller than the Eiffel Tower in Paris, France, but it was never finished.

Great Victorian Way (1855)

A railway, roads and buildings – all under glass – was to circle around London for 19 kilometres.

Crystal Tower (1851)

This was to be made by tilting the 1851 Great Exhibition hall, in Hyde Park, onto its side.

Trafalgar Square Pyramid (1815)

Would have been 91 metres – taller than St Paul's Cathedral – with 22 levels

The grand Pantheon of Oxford Street (1772–1937)

The world-famous St James's Theatre (1835–1957)

Here are some superb city landmarks that would still be here today, had they not been battered by the wrecking ball..!

The Duke of Northumberland's London townhouse (1605–1874)

The Egyptian Hall of Piccadilly (1812–1905)

Over the years, many interesting buildings have been designed to add to **London's skyline** – but some of them were never built. If they had been, the city's skyline might now look completely different!

HIGH CUISINE:
On 23 October 1843, 14 stonemasons – who had been constructing Nelson's Column (right) – had a meal on the platform at the very top. This was just before the statue of Admiral Nelson was added to it.

St Paul's Stone Pineapple (1666)
One design for the Cathedral's dome had an 18-metre-high pineapple-shaped sculpture at the top.

Elevated Railway (1840s)
This was intended to run along the Thames between London Bridge and Charing Cross.

Crystal Tower Bridge (1940s)
The idea was to put Tower Bridge inside a huge glass case. As you can see, it never happened.

Greenwich Park Britannia (1799)
A 70-metre-tall statue of 'Britannia' was suggested. It would've looked out over the Thames.

DEEP-LEVEL SHELTERS
Eight shelters, very **deep underground,** were used to store important equipment and government workers during the London air raids of the Second World War (see page 9). They were built beneath Tube stations, and their entrances are still visible at street level. See if you can find them!

North London

South London

- Belsize Park
- Camden Town
- Goodge Street
- Chancery Lane
- Stockwell
- Clapham North
- Clapham Common
- Clapham South

Weird London

There are lots of weird and wonderful things about the city of London. You'll hear some 'urban legends' that might not be true, but there are also many cast-iron London facts that are just plain strange!

London, Ohio, USA

London, Ontario, Canada

London, Nigeria

London, Equatorial Guinea

London, Kentucky, USA

London, Christmas Island

London, Belize

Proud Londoners will tell you that there's "Only one London" – but in fact this isn't true! There are **more than 30 different places named London** around the planet. Here's just a few of them.

In the 1930s, a ghostly bus was sometimes seen speeding past a dangerous junction in Ladbroke Grove, West London. The sightings stopped after this section of road was rebuilt.

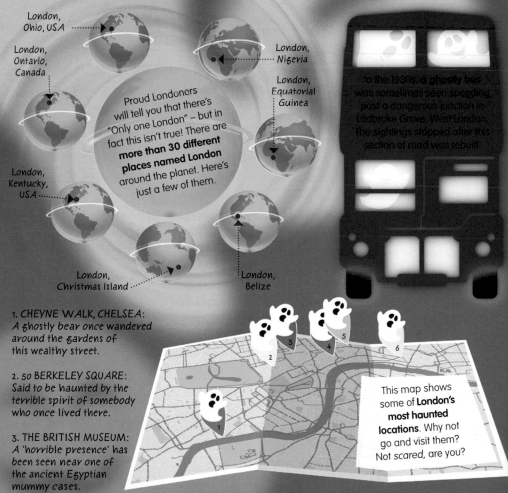

1. CHEYNE WALK, CHELSEA: A ghostly bear once wandered around the gardens of this wealthy street.

2. 50 BERKELEY SQUARE: Said to be haunted by the terrible spirit of somebody who once lived there.

3. THE BRITISH MUSEUM: A 'horrible presence' has been seen near one of the ancient Egyptian mummy cases.

4. THEATRE ROYAL, DRURY LANE: Haunted by 'The Man in Grey', the ghost of an actor who was murdered at the theatre.

5. UNIVERSITY COLLEGE HOSPITAL, GOWER ST: Haunted by the unhappy spirit of a nurse.

6. THE BANK OF ENGLAND, THREADNEEDLE ST: The ghost of a bank clerk, called William Jenkins, continued to walk the corridors of the building after he died.

This map shows some of **London's most haunted locations**. Why not go and visit them? Not scared, are you?

LOST PROPERTY

London's passengers can be frighteningly forgetful! Here are ten of the most **weird and wonderful objects** that have ended up in London Transport's Lost Property offices over the years.

London is famous for its rainy and changeable weather – but here are some of the more **unusual weather events** that have hit the capital over the years.

125 kg of sultanas

Coffin from a theatre show

Lawnmower

Stuffed eagle

4.25-metres-long boat

Park bench

Garden slide

Dead bats

Bed

Human skulls

30 October 1091:
THE LONDON TORNADO

26–27 November 1703:
LONDON'S WORST-EVER STORM

8 March 1750:
AN EARTHQUAKE!

6–7 JANUARY 1928:
FLOOD! THE THAMES BURSTS ITS BANKS

The following Londoners were still seen around the city **after they'd died**. Their bodies were either embalmed or otherwise preserved – as mummies!

The naturally preserved body of 'Jimmy Garlick' was discovered under the floor of a church, in the City of London, in 1839.

December 1952:
THE DEADLY INDUSTRIAL SMOG (that killed around 4,000 people)

15–16 October 1987:
BRITAIN'S LAST MAJOR STORM

Catherine of Valois was the queen of King Henry V. She died in 1437, aged 35. Her embalmed body was put on public display for more than 200 years, until 1776.

Mr J Bentham

Jeremy Bentham, a 19th-century philosopher, left his body to be put on display at University College London. His skeleton is dressed in his own clothes, with a waxwork of his head perched on top. The real head, which is mummified, is kept in a locked box nearby.

Yes, it's me!

Festive city

London is a city of celebration, where festivals take place all year round. Some of these are public events, while others are cultural or religious festivals that are also held all over the world. Here are some of the events that attract the most visitors.

500,000 SPECTATORS USUALLY FLOCK TO THE THAMES TO SEE THE NEW YEAR DISPLAYS

31 December–1 January:
NEW YEAR'S EVE

London usually ushers in the new year with a **spectacular fireworks show**. The main display normally takes place at the Victoria Embankment, overlooking the Thames, with many of the fireworks launched from the wheel of the London Eye – often in time to a loud, fast-paced, musical sound track.

COST OF FIREWORKS: **£313,000** (MORE THAN £500 PER SECOND)

CITY HALL: meeting place of the London Assembly.

30 ST MARY AXE: also known as The Gherkin building.

September:
OPEN HOUSE LONDON

This is an annual festival where visitors get the chance to explore **famous and fascinating buildings** (or locations) that aren't normally open to the public. It's a great chance to get inside and learn all about London's hidden treasures.

10 DOWNING STREET: the main residence of British Prime Ministers since 1735.

BT TOWER: broadcast, internet and telephone information is beamed out from here.

15,000 FEATHER PLUMES are used in the costumes

1 MILLION HOURS needed to make and decorate all the costumes

Around **80–300** PERFORMERS in each 'Mas band'

August:
THE NOTTING HILL CARNIVAL

The Notting Hill Carnival, held for one weekend each August in West London, is **Europe's biggest public street party**. People go to experience the loud music and the amazing costumes worn by the performers of the 'Mas' (masquerade) bands.

30 MILLION SEQUINS in all the costumes

January–February:
CHINESE NEW YEAR

There are more than 107,000 British Chinese people living in London. Altogether, **up to 500,000 people gather** in Central London – and in the city's own Chinatown – to celebrate the Chinese New Year, otherwise known as the Spring Festival.

NEW MOON

FULL MOON

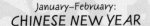

In China, the months follow their Lunar Calendar, which changes according to the cycle of the Moon. This means the Chinese New Year may fall anywhere between 21 January and 20 February.

May:
THE CHELSEA FLOWER SHOW

11,775 SQUARE METRES is the amount of space covered by the show's Great Pavilion ...

... which is enough room to park **500** LONDON BUSES

This week-long event has been held most years since 1913, usually at the end of May. Amazing 'display gardens' are set up so that visitors can see plants, flowers and **garden designs from all over the planet**.

SOMETIMES, MORE THAN **12,000** WORKS OF ART ARE SENT IN

ARTISTS CAN SEND IN DIGITAL PICTURES OF THEIR WORK TO THE ACADEMY'S SELECTORS

UP TO **£70,000** WORTH OF PRIZES ARE AWARDED TO ARTISTS

AROUND **1,100** ARTWORKS, OR MORE, CAN BE CHOSEN FOR DISPLAY

June:
THE SUMMER EXHIBITION

THOUSANDS OF THE ARTWORKS GET SOLD TO ART LOVERS EACH YEAR

The Royal Academy's Summer Exhibition is an art show where anybody can send in their work, in the hope that it might be chosen and put on display. It's **the largest 'open' exhibition of its kind** in the whole world.

CARNIVAL SPECTATORS

400,000 TOURISTS

1.6 MILLION LONDONERS

Up to **2** MILLION people go to see the Notting Hill Carnival.

London: more things to find

Going to London once is never enough! You'll need to make many visits to make the most of such an enormous, ever-changing place. Here are some things to look up – or look out for – on your travels.

REALLY USEFUL WEBSITES
Get ahead of the game in the big city. Before you visit a museum or gallery, or go to an event, it's a good idea to find out what's there to see or do. That way, you won't miss out on the very best stuff!

Historic London

The London Monument, City of London: *www.themonument.info*
Museum of London, 150 London Wall, London EC2Y 5HN: *www.museumoflondon.org.uk/london-wall*
St Paul's Cathedral: *www.stpauls.co.uk*
Tower Bridge: *www.towerbridge.org.uk*
The Tower of London: *www.hrp.org.uk/tower-of-london*
Westminster Abbey: *www.westminster-abbey.org*
Westminster and the UK Parliament: *www.parliament.uk*

Cultural London

The British Museum, Great Russell Street, London WC1B 3DG: *www.britishmuseum.org*
The Natural History Museum, Cromwell Road, London SW7 5BD: *www.nhm.ac.uk*
The Open House London Festival: *www.openhouselondon.org.uk*
The Royal Albert Hall, Kensington Gore, London SW7 2AP: *www.royalalberthall.com*
Sir John Soane's Museum, 13 Lincoln's Inn Fields, London WC2A 3BP: *www.soane.org*
The Victoria and Albert Museum, Cromwell Road, London SW7 2RL: *www.vam.ac.uk*

Arty London

The National Gallery, Trafalgar Square, London WC2N 5DN: *www.nationalgallery.org.uk*
The National Portrait Gallery, St Martin's Place, London WC2H 0HE: *www.npg.org.uk*
The Royal Academy of Arts, Burlington House, Piccadilly, London W1J 0BD: *www.royalacademy.org.uk*
The Tate Galleries (in London and elsewhere): *www.tate.org.uk/art*

Fictional London

The Sherlock Holmes Museum, 221B Baker Street, London NW1 6XE: *www.sherlock-holmes.co.uk*

Science and transport in London

The London Transport Museum, Covent Garden Piazza, London WC2E 7BB: *www.ltmuseum.co.uk*
Science Museum, Exhibition Road, London SW7 2DD: *www.sciencemuseum.org.uk*
The Thames Barrier, 1 Unity Way, London SE18 5NJ: *www.gov.uk/guidance/the-thames-barrier*

Royal London

Royal events (including Trooping the Colour, the Queen's official birthday):
www.royal.gov.uk/royaleventsandceremonies/overview.aspx

Green and wild London

London's Royal Parks: *www.royalparks.org.uk*
The city's wildlife: *www.wildlondon.org.uk*
ZSL London Zoo, Regent's Park, London NW1 4RY: *www.zsl.org/zsl-london-zoo*

High-altitude London

The London Eye, South Bank, London SE1 7PB: *www.londoneye.com*
The Shard, 32 London Bridge Street, London SE1 9SG: *www.the-shard.com*

Sporty London

The annual Oxford-Cambridge boat races: *http://theboatraces.org*
The Wimbledon tennis championships: *www.wimbledon.com*

CITY STORES WORTH VISITING

Daunt Books, 83 Marylebone High Street, London W1U: *www.dauntbooks.co.uk*
Fortnum and Mason, 181 Piccadilly, London W1A 1ER: *www.fortnumandmason.com*
Foyles, 107 Charing Cross Road, London WC2H 0DT: *www.foyles.co.uk/bookstore-charing-cross*
Hamleys, 188–196 Regent St, London W1B 5BT: *www.hamleys.com*
Harrods, 87–135 Brompton Road, Knightsbridge, London, SW1X 7XL: *www.harrods.com*
Selfridges & Co, 400 Oxford Street, London, W1A 1AB www.selfridges.com
Waterstones, 203–206 Piccadilly, London, W1J 9HD: *www.waterstones.com/bookshops/piccadilly*

UNUSUAL PLACES

You don't always have to follow the crowds! Here are a few things to look out for on your own,
personal London Treasure Hunt:
Can you find the statue of PETER PAN in the Kensington Gardens?
How about the last remaining fragments of the LONDON STONE in Cannon Street?
Do you fancy seeing a show at the PUPPET THEATRE BARGE, which is moored in Little Venice?

ROAMING FURTHER AFIELD

There are also some fantastic places on the outskirts of London, or just outside the city, such as:
Hampton Court Palace, East Molesey, Surrey KT8 9AU: www.hrp.org.uk/hampton-court-palace
The Horniman Museum, 100 London Rd, Forest Hill, London SE23 3PQ: http://www.horniman.ac.uk
The London Wetland Centre, Queen Elizabeth's Walk, Barnes, London SW13 9WT:
www.wwt.org.uk/wetland-centres/london

Index